Bird's-Eye View

Story by Jenny Giles

Illustrations by Rachel Tonkin

Luke sat in the cab
of his father's truck
and looked down
at the truck garage.

It was Saturday morning,
and he could see
some of the drivers
cleaning their trucks.
Others were busy loading up
and getting ready for a long drive.

4

Luke loved trucks,
and he came to the garage
with his father every Saturday.

"Move over, Luke," said Dad,
as he jumped up into the cab.
"I'm going to take the truck
out into the lot.
I have to check all the tires."

Luke moved across the seat,
and Dad started the engine.
He drove the truck slowly
out into the lot.

"I can see everything
from up here, Dad," said Luke.
"Houses, roads, people...
and a new building!"

Dad smiled.
"We have a bird's-eye view," he said.
"Do you know what that is, Luke?"

Luke looked up at the sky.
"Birds can see everything
when they are flying," he said,
"so when I look down there,
I've got a bird's-eye view!"

"Right!" said Dad. "And now
you can keep an eye on things
while I check the tires."

Luke looked down at the houses.
He could see children playing
and people walking up and down.
Then he saw a little girl
running down the road,
toward the building site.

Luke watched the little girl
go in the gate.
He saw her run behind the shed
and go to play in a pile of sand.

Soon, Luke saw some people
running up and down the street.
They were calling out
and looking over fences.

An older boy came up the steps
to the truck garage.
"Have you seen a little girl?"
he asked.
"We can't find my sister anywhere!"

"I think I know where she is,"
called Luke.
"There's a little girl
down by the new building.
She's playing in the sand.
You can't see her from the road,
because she's behind the shed."

Luke showed the boy
where the little girl was.
"That's her!" shouted the boy,
and he ran back to his father.

Luke and Dad
went down the steps.
They watched
the little girl's father
run behind the shed.

He picked up the little girl
and came back with her.

Then everyone thanked Luke.
"We couldn't see her anywhere!"
they said.

"I could see her," said Luke,
"because I was sitting up there
in Dad's truck. I had a
bird's-eye view of everything!"